M000188803

A CLEAR SIGHT ACADEMIC PRESS EDITION

Nonprofit Financial Leadership

A QUICK START GUIDE

Brian Daniel

Clear Sight Academic Press, New York, NY

First edition.

ISBN: 978-0-692-74221-1

TABLE OF CONTENTS

ACKNOWLEDGEMENTS

Many people from many organizations and backgrounds helped me develop the thinking behind this book.

The Knowledge

Thanks to my colleagues on the senior team at the NYC Lesbian and Gay Community Center:

> **Glennda Testone,** Executive Director
>
> **Rob Wheeler,** Chief Operating Officer
>
> **Carrie Davis,** Chief Program Officer
>
> **Jeffrey Klein,** Chief Development Officer

First they taught me, then they listened patiently as I figured it out. Then they encouraged me.

The Bigger Concept

Thanks to **Cynthia Thompson, Ph.D.**, Academic Director of the Executive MBA program and Professor in the Department of Management at the Zicklin School of Business at Baruch College in New York City.

Thanks also to **Gwendolyn Webb**, **Ph.D.**, Executive Director of Executive Programs and Academic Director of the Executive MS Program in Finance at the Zicklin School of Business.

The Book

I cannot thank enough the two people who made themselves available, read every draft, and remained cheerful throughout my writing process, **William P. Grundy** and **Maria Douaihy**. Profound thanks!

I received a huge amount of pleasant helpfulness from my editor, **Jill Bailin**. The images and the cover originated in my mind and were beautifully realized by graphic designer **Ray Cabarga.** Thank you both for your incredibly professional support!

My Backstops

Eternal thanks to my ever supportive family: **Wilson, Oscar**, and **Cupid.**

Finally the biggest thanks of all to my dad, **Robert**, who instilled in me the desires to work hard and be helpful. I am doing my best.

About the Author

BRIAN DANIEL is the president and principal advisor of Clear Sight Advisors, a financial coaching and advisory firm focused on nonprofit executives and board directors. Brian has an MBA and more than 30 years of executive, finance, and accounting experience in a wide array of industries, including nonprofit organizations. He is an adjunct professor of accounting in the Executive MBA program at Baruch College in New York City.

INTRODUCTION

I want to start by wishing you, the reader of this book, a hearty "congratulations"! In fact, you are due more than one. First, you have succeeded in becoming the leader of your organization, or in participating on the board. To be entrusted with either of these roles signifies that you have shown deep passion for your nonprofit, and also that you are respected for your capabilities. Second, you have picked up this book. You are on your way to becoming a financial leader of your nonprofit organization. You are the reason that I wrote this book, and helping you to constantly improve your financial leadership is the goal of my work. Before moving on, here's a bit about the book itself and how it came about.

The Notion of a "Quick Start Guide"

This year I bought a new wireless music speaker for my home. Here's something I understand about myself: I am not a technology expert. Given this known knowledge gap, I still plunged ahead with the purchase. When I opened the box I found two sets of instructions. The first, a thick, somewhat intimidating, densely typed set of "instructions," and second, a thin, plastic-coated and colorful "quick start" guide.

I opted immediately for the quick start guide. Why? All I wanted or needed to know was the basics of how to use the new speaker. I needed to know what the buttons were for, how to turn it on and off, and how to take care of it. I knew that there was much more to learn from the "instructions," but I didn't have time for that level of learning. Also, I knew that if needed there would be an expert who could assist me. The detailed technical information is just not for me or my needs. They exist for someone, just not me.

This Book

The purpose of the "quick start guide" you are now holding in your hands is similar to what I described above. It is for people who have willingly decided to be financial leaders, yet do not have the time or the need to learn nonprofit accounting in all its detailed glory. A multitude of very good books exist for the accountants on our boards and in our organizations. However, this guide is specifically for nonprofit executives and board directors who have fiduciary or management oversight responsibilities, but do not have detailed knowledge of nonprofit accounting. My experience tells me this "quick start" guide will help you become a more effective, financially literate leader of your organization. This in turn will help you lead your organization toward becoming a tighter, more well-managed nonprofit.

Written for You

For the new or incumbent board director, if you are like most board members, you were recruited to the board for specific reasons: you are passionate about the organization's mission, you have a network of potential sources of funding for the organization, you have specific skillsets related to current or future programs, or many other possible reasons. For all the talents and skills you bring to your new board position, financial management skills may not be among them. However, recognizing your role and fiduciary responsibilities, this book is geared to help you make a quick leap toward becoming a financial leader today.

For the new or long-term executive director, you are the leading executive of your nonprofit organization, one with which you share passion and mission alignment, for which you have ideas for new programs and growth, and you are ready to meet the fundraising needs to make this happen. Of all the skills and energy you bring to your role, you may be lacking financial expertise, and will soon be relying on a staff to help you understand your financial situation and make important decisions. This book is for you. It is designed with your needs in mind, and geared toward helping you be a financial leader today.

The Path We are Going to Take—Together

Think of this as an immersion course. We are going to take a deep breath and dive into the four primary financial statements required for all nonprofits. When we dive in, we'll:

- Define the purpose of each statement and take a look at its visual layout

- Discuss the columns and rows, and learn to read the information on the statements

- Learn how to analyze the financial statements

- Using financial statements for a fictional nonprofit, prepare to explain the results of your organization to key stakeholders, or to raise questions about results

- Learn about my "secret sauce," a summary tool of the analytical techniques that can be the foundation of your financial dashboard

Get ready

If I can ask for another wish (you already have the book), I'd ask you to actually use this book, not just read it. When you are preparing to move to the first chapter *(the Statement of Activities)*, print a copy of the most recent audited statements for your organization and keep them within reach of this book. I believe you will truly amplify your learning if you travel between this book and your own statements regularly. Also, do not fear a calculator. Try some of the simple calculations using your own financial information. Let's work together through this process, so that with each page you turn, you will have learned more about your nonprofit.

The book is primarily arranged by financial statement, with a chapter devoted to each. The last chapter will have some additional, more detailed accounting information that you might find useful. There is also a list of vocabulary terms, and a set of additional internal management reports in the appendix. Finally, please visit the book's companion website at **www.clearsightadvisors.co/premium** to download and print all the statements found in the book.

Before moving to chapter 1, here is a diagram that might be helpful as a reference as we move forward. The relationships among the four statements in time, and to each other, will be a recurring theme throughout the book.

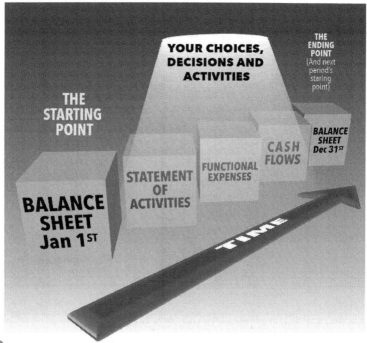

The Statement of Activities

(ALSO KNOWN AS THE INCOME STATEMENT)

Overview

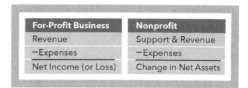

This simple comparison chart shows how both for-profit and nonprofit organizations calculate their operating performance.

What is it, and What is it Used For?

The Statement of Activities reports an organization's revenues and expenses for a specific range of time. In the world of "for-profit" business, this statement is known as the Income Statement. In addition to reporting the revenues and expenses, this statement also has a *bottom line,* called the *change in net assets.* Change in net assets is the same as *net income.* Since we are embarking on a learning experience, I will use these terms interchangeably throughout this chapter and the book, just as happens in the real world.

Through reporting revenues and expenses over a period of time, we report the operating activities of the organization. We will consider additional key forms of reporting in subsequent chapters.

Let's Break it Down

Throughout this book, we will use sample statements for a fictitious nonprofit called All Good People, Inc., also known as AGP. Note: The financial information for All Good People,

Inc. is completely fictional and only presented here as a learning tool. Keep this in mind while you learn. Your organization's statements are the best tool for your comprehension of these new concepts. AGP's Income Statement for its fiscal year ended June 30, 2015 is shown below.

ALL GOOD PEOPLE, INC.
Statement of Activities
Fiscal Year Ended June 30, 2015
(with totals for the year ended June 30, 2014)

REVENUE AND SUPPORT	UNRESTRICTED	TEMPORARILY RESTRICTED	2015 TOTAL	2014 TOTAL
Fundraising events revenue, net of expenses ($125,000 in 2015 and $110,000 in 2014)	$ 1,550,000	$	$ 1,550,000	$ 1,425,000
Government grants	3,096,000		3,096,000	3,105,000
Contributions	325,000	1,210,000	1,535,000	1,460,000
In-kind contributions	75,000		75,000	
Net assets released from restrictions	1,397,000	(1,397,000)		
Total Revenue and Support	6,443,000	(187,000)	6,256,000	5,990,000
EXPENSES				
Program services	4,619,000		4,619,000	4,511,000
Supporting Services				
Management and general	717,000		717,000	695,000
Fundraising	1,068,000		1,068,000	758,000
Total Supporting Services	1,785,000		1,785,000	1,453,000
Total Expenses	6,404,000		6,404,000	5,964,000
Change in Net Assets	39,000	(187,000)	(148,000)	26,000
NET ASSETS				
Beginning of year	2,566,000	464,000	3,030,000	13,004,000
End of year	$ 2,605,000	$ 277,000	$ 2,882,000	$ 13,030,000

First, let's examine the title of the report, as well as the column headers.

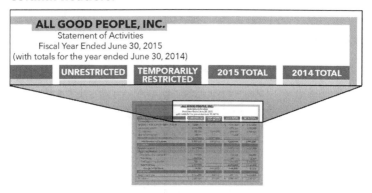

The title includes the organization's name *(All Good People, Inc.)*, the type of report *(Statement of Activities)*, and the dates covered by the report *(fiscal year ended June 30, 2015)*. As mentioned previously, the time period for the Statement of Activities is a range of dates, typically given as a month, quarter, or year. For internal reporting, some organizations also create this statement on a weekly basis.

For our sample organization, we can see that the statement reflects activities for the fiscal year, ended June 30, 2015. For purposes of comparison, it also shows results for the prior year, ended June 30, 2014. As we will see, the ability to compare between years is one of the most powerful features of the Income Statement.

For the current year's results, the statement also gives additional critical details about restricted and unrestricted funds. Many, though not all, gifts made to a nonprofit organization come with strings attached. Those strings are also known as restrictions. The columns labeled "Unrestricted" and "Temporarily Restricted" are critical indicators of an organization's effectiveness at fundraising and deploying grantor funds according to their stated purposes. As discussed further below, this format also makes clear the amount of newly received restricted grants, as well as funds being released from restriction, a key relationship that speaks to the near-term future of the organization. Let's define each column.

Unrestricted funds have no strings attached. Board or management can allocate these funds for any organizational purpose. An example is a $2,000 gift made to the organization with no other information. Such a gift can be used in any way determined by the organization, including to cover general operating expenses.

Temporarily Restricted is the column where you'll find other grants that come to your organization for a specific purpose. As I mentioned earlier, if a donor places a restriction on a gift, it must be used exactly in accordance with the donor's wishes, often for specific programmatic purposes. It is important to keep in mind that a restriction can be defined by *purpose* or by *time*. A $5,000 grant for adult counseling services is an example of a grant restricted by purpose, while a $3,000 grant for use over two years is restricted by time.

Some organizations will also have a column called **Permanently Restricted.** For permanently restricted funds, the principal amount of the gift must be retained in whole in perpetuity, meaning they cannot be used in any way that will diminish the original value of the gift. Additionally, these types of gifts tend to come with other provisions, such as conditions on the use of earnings from investment of the funds. Although permanently restricted gifts place constraints on spending, they provide an organization with a perpetual source of funding, through annual earnings on the investment of the principal.

The final column shows data from the **prior year.** External statements (those prepared by the auditors, for example) will always show results from the previous year, allowing management and the board to highlight changes across time. Internal financial statements (those that staff and the board use for management purposes) will likely also include a budget column, allowing them to ensure that the organization is operating according to the previously approved plan.

The Rows

Now that we understand the columns on the Income Statement, let's turn to the rows. The rows display three main sections of the Income Statement formula: revenues, expenses, and change in net assets. **Revenue** is the money that came into the organization during the designated time period. **Expenses**, as you have guessed, details the money that has left the organization during the same period. And **change in net assets** is what remains after subtracting expenses from revenue.

What Is "Revenue and Support"?

Revenue and support includes the various ways an organization generates the funding it needs to provide its mission-related services. Without complicating the issue, we are not talking about direct payments of cash here, although the activities listed under revenue and support will ultimately result in cash for the organization. We will come back to this issue in chapters 3 and 4. For now let's accept the idea that we can have revenue that may or may not be cash.

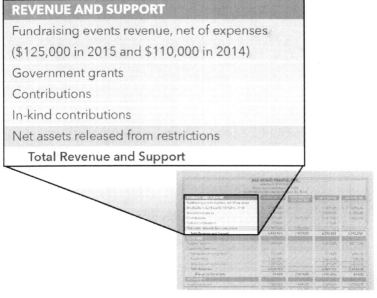

REVENUE AND SUPPORT

Fundraising events revenue, net of expenses ($125,000 in 2015 and $110,000 in 2014)

Government grants

Contributions

In-kind contributions

Net assets released from restrictions

    Total Revenue and Support

Revenues are generated when a product or service is exchanged for payment. Examples are ticket sales for a performance, or insurance payments made for client services. **Support**, on the other hand, relates to funds contributed to the organization without anything expected in return. There are several types of revenue and support, depending on the type of organization. Defined below are some common types of support.

Most nonprofit organizations host *fundraising events*, such as periodic galas, both to recognize and engage their supporters and to raise funds. To provide transparency over the organization's overall cost of fundraising, this amount is typically shown *net of event expenses.* I will return to this idea shortly.

Government grants (or contracts) are provided by government agencies at the local, state, and federal levels. These agencies make funds available for specific purposes at specific times, and winning them usually requires the submission of detailed RFPs. If your organization has government contracts, the amount of reimbursed costs are reflected in this row.

Contributions are gifts made to the organization either through normal fundraising appeals or as unsolicited donations. The contributions row also includes foundation and corporate grants, which are typically made as temporarily restricted funds. Many organizations cultivate long-term relationships with these types of funders both to lower annual fundraising costs and increase the likelihood of consistent future support. It is important to note that contributions must meet specific accounting criteria to be reported as support. I will return in a later chapter to the term for these contributions, namely *unconditional promises to give*.

In-kind contributions are services or goods that have been provided to your organization on a *pro bono* (free!) basis. These can include a wide range of offerings, including legal (or other professional) fees, or food products for a fundraising event, or a drug company's donations toward combating disease. The fair market value of donated goods or services is included as revenue. The same amount of expense is also included in the appropriate expense row of the statement. This accounting convention results in no net effect on the bottom line, but permits the costs of running the organization to be correctly reflected.

Net assets released from restrictions is a key term for us. Donors often give money to a nonprofit organization with specific requirements for its use. As we have seen, these restrictions can either be delineated by purpose or by time. In releasing funds from restriction, the organization is stating that it has fulfilled its commitment to the donor. Such a statement has both legal and financial implications and should be made only after careful deliberation. Financial leaders must ensure that their accounting practices track expenses for each of the restricted grants your organization receives. This is the best way to ensure that funds are spent according to a donor's original wishes, and not incorrectly spent elsewhere.

What Are Expenses?

Expenses represent the money the organization spends. This statement shows expenses in three major functional categories: *program services, management and general*, and *fundraising*. A more detailed list of expense categories will be discussed later.

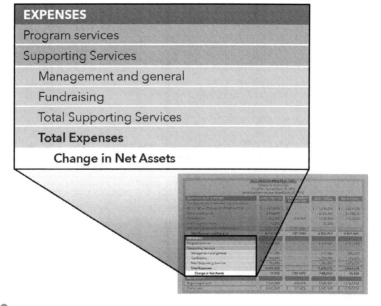

Programs services expenses are costs directly related to the organization's mission. Most donors want all of their funds allocated to direct, mission-related spending. Think of this row as the way an organization measures its efficiency in using donated funds. This is also where most of an organization's restricted funding is applied.

Management and general expenses are incurred by even the most efficient organization. These include, at a minimum, costs for the executive director, accounting, year-end audits, technology, and administrative expenses. Management and administrative expenses typically require unrestricted forms of funding.

Fundraising is the cost of generating the revenue and support described previously. As noted above, these expenses do not include the direct costs of fundraising events or galas. They do, however, include all other costs related to fundraising activity, such as staffing costs, email campaigns, and donor appreciation events.

Program expenses are often called direct expenses, reflecting their direct application to programmatic services. In contrast, management and fundraising expenses are often called supporting or indirect expenses, reflecting their use in providing the necessary organizational capacity that spans individual programs and initiatives.

What Is Change in Net Assets?

Change in net assets is an organization's net income, profit, or bottom line. This value is the result of subtracting the organization's expenses from its revenue and support.

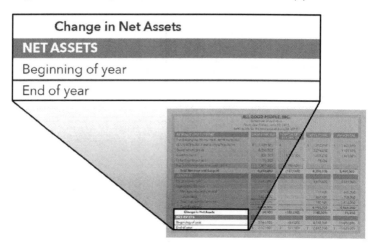

Change in Net Assets	
NET ASSETS	
Beginning of year	
End of year	

The notion of "profit" can be a particular quandary for board and management. Should a nonprofit generate profit (a positive change in net assets)? It's complicated, but yes. Yes, because a positive bottom line does a couple of important things over the long run: it can help to build a reserve fund (savings for the inevitable rainy day), and it can also enable management and the board to introduce new programming. However, an occasionally negative bottom line is not necessarily harmful to a nonprofit organization. This could happen, for example, during a period when the organization deliberately elects to use its previously created reserve.

Still, both for-profit and nonprofit organizations alike must generate enough positive bottom line over time to sustain themselves.

Let's consider that last comment. Generally speaking, restricted donations and government grants pay for program services, not for administration and fundraising costs. Administration and fundraising costs need to be funded through unrestricted fundraising. So, if the unrestricted fundraising goals are not met, it usually means that some of the administration or fundraising costs must be reduced. Therefore, in order to ensure that you are able to cover all of your costs over time, a positive bottom line will build a reserve to help alleviate stress when unrestricted fundraising goals are not being met.

The last several rows of the Income Statement show what I call the *balance roll-forward of net assets*. Here, we begin to introduce the concept of balances, which I will discuss in detail when we get to the Statement of Financial Position in chapter 3. For the purposes of wrapping up this statement, however, notice that you can see both the cumulative balance of net assets (for each column), and how much each balance has changed during the period of the statement. More learning about balances coming soon!

What do the Numbers Mean, and How Do They Relate to Each Other?

Take a look at the sample Statement of Activities, with particular focus on the current year. It is made up of three columns. Let's discuss how to use the information in each.

We start with the **bottom line** (change in net assets) and ask ourselves whether it's positive or negative, and how it's different in each column. Let's remind ourselves of the simple equation:

Change in Net Assets = Total Revenue – Total Expenses

THE FIRST COLUMN, "Unrestricted," is the operating performance of the organization for the time period of the report. It represents all of the sources of general revenue and support, and how those funds were used. As we discussed earlier, the bottom line should normally be positive. That means the organization received more revenues than it spent. While the mission of a nonprofit is not to generate profits, prudent management should lead toward regular profits, helping establish a reserve for future, unplanned needs. In the case of All Good People, the organization generated a positive change in net assets of $39,000 during the year.

THE SECOND COLUMN, "Temporarily Restricted," shows how much in new, temporarily restricted grants the organization received during the period ($1,210,000), as well as the amount of temporarily restricted funds *released from restriction* ($1,397,000), resulting in a negative change in net assets of $187,000 for the year. Just a reminder that when the organization has fulfilled its commitment to the donor, temporarily restricted net assets are released from restriction. This column will vary between positive and negative change in net assets, depending upon the period's fundraising success. Although an occasional negative value in this column is understandable, successive periods of negative change in net assets in this column means that temporarily restricted funds are being depleted more rapidly than they are being raised. This could quickly jeopardize the sustainability of the organization's program offerings and the fulfillment of its mission.

THE THIRD COLUMN for the current period is a total of the first two. This total represents the financial activity of the organization as a whole. Although this figure is important, the first two columns provide more actionable information for financial leaders.

Now let's compare the results between the years (or between budget and actuals, if a budget is available). This is called horizontal analysis, as we are comparing data across the rows.

$ variance = current period – prior period

On its own, results from the current period are informative, but it is always helpful to compare them to something else, whether a prior period or a budget. By doing this, you can observe changes from what has previously happened, or what was expected to happen. In both cases, a financial leader armed with this information can ask appropriate questions or make informed decisions. As an example, fundraising event revenue increased $125,000, to $1,550,000, from 2014 to 2015.

You can also show the change as a percent:

$$\% \ variance = \frac{\$ \ variance}{prior \ period}$$

Continuing with our sample statements, fundraising revenue increased by $125,000, or 8.8% from the previous year.

Now let's compare items within a column to each other. This is called a margin or vertical analysis. In a vertical analysis, we are only comparing the items that exist within a single column.

Net margin is one of the most important indicators of financial performance: profitability. This is the relationship between an organization's revenue and its bottom line, and gives an indication of its sustainability in the near future. You can calculate net margin by dividing the change in net assets by the total revenue of the same column. The resulting percentage tells you how much of every dollar of revenue was added to (or used from) the organization's reserve (unrestricted) and/or temporarily unrestricted net assets.

$$\text{net margin} = \frac{\text{change in net assets}}{\text{total support and revenue}}$$

Similarly we can compare each **functional** expense to total expenses. We will get in to the details of each of these categories in the next chapter, so think of this as a foundation before we move ahead.

$$\text{program spending \%} = \frac{\text{program expenses}}{\text{total expenses}}$$

$$\text{management spending \%} = \frac{\text{management expenses}}{\text{total expenses}}$$

$$\text{fundraising spending \%} = \frac{\text{fundraising expenses}}{\text{total expenses}}$$

These three functional ratios measure how much of each dollar spent goes toward the organization's mission (program), management/administrative costs, and fundraising. Funders of nonprofits invariably seek high results for program services, as a key indicator for how dollars are spent in fulfillment of the organization's mission. A general threshold suggests that 65-70% of an organization's spending should be dedicated to programs. With this in mind, it is important to note that this ratio is one of many data points to be used in analyzing successful mission alignment. This ratio is most important to measure over time: Is the organization spending more or less of its overall expense on programming?

Finally, each type of revenue can be compared to total revenue. This allows us to observe changes in the makeup of different types of revenues. The ratios given below are important to organizations with varied sources of income, as each source of revenue and support typically requires a different type of fundraising expertise or activity. Dramatic changes to the makeup of revenues can require changes to the fundraising capacity of the organization. Here's how this works:

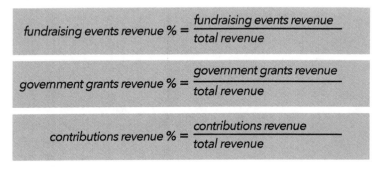

$$\text{fundraising events revenue \%} = \frac{\text{fundraising events revenue}}{\text{total revenue}}$$

$$\text{government grants revenue \%} = \frac{\text{government grants revenue}}{\text{total revenue}}$$

$$\text{contributions revenue \%} = \frac{\text{contributions revenue}}{\text{total revenue}}$$

An important consideration for every nonprofit is its **cost of fundraising**. Specifically, how can an organization measure the effectiveness of its fundraising expenditures? One way that I have found useful is to compare total fundraising expenses to revenues raised by the development team.

$$\text{fundraising effectiveness, total} = \frac{\text{total revenues}}{\text{fundraising expenses}}$$

The measure can be read as "$'s of revenue generated for each $ spent on fundraising." Take liberties with this concept. For example, if your development team is not responsible for government grants, we wouldn't include the government revenues in the measure. The adjusted formula would be:

$$\text{fundraising effectiveness, excluding govt. grants} = \frac{\text{total revenues - govt. grants}}{\text{fundraising expenses}}$$

Now that we have covered several margin calculations (within each vertical column), something powerful becomes available to us. Similar to comparing the dollar results against prior periods or budget, each of the ratios and calculations can be compared to prior periods and budgets. Armed with this information, the financial leader can make intuitive, reasoned assessments, and probe more deeply into the significant areas of change.

Building a Narrative

Below I have written a narrative based on the sample Statement of Activities presented here. Our example organization, All Good People, has just completed the annual audit that produced this Statement of Activities. As a financial leader, you have the responsibility of explaining the statement to an audience, perhaps board members. The following is an assessment of the organization's results using the techniques I described above.

ALL GOOD PEOPLE, INC.

Statement of Activities

Fiscal Year Ended June 30, 2015

(with totals for the year ended June 30, 2014)

	2015 Total	2014 Total	2014 vs 2015 $	2014 vs 2015 %
REVENUE AND SUPPORT				A
Fundraising events revenue, net of expenses ($125,000 in 2015 and $110,000 in 2014)	$ 1,550,000	$ 1,425,000	$ 125,000	8.8%
Government grants	3,096,000	3,105,000	(9,000)	-0.3%
Contributions	1,535,000	1,460,000	75,000	5.1%
In-kind contributions	75,000		75,000	n/m
Net assets released from restrictions				n/m
Total Revenue and Support	6,256,000	5,990,000	266,000	4.4%
EXPENSES				C
Program services	4,619,000	4,511,000	(108,000)	-2.4%
Supporting Services				
Management and general	717,000	695,000	(22,000)	-3.2%
Fundraising	1,068,000	758,000	(310,000)	-40.9%
Total Supporting Services	1,785,000	1,453,000	(332,000)	-22.8%
Total Expense	6,404,000	5,964,000	(440,000)	-7.4%
Change in Net Assets	$ (148,000)	26,000	(174,000)	-669.2%

NET ASSETS

Beginning of year		3,030,000	13,004,000
End of year	$ 2,882,000	$ 13,030,000
Net margin	**-2.4%**	**0.4%** F

MIX OF FUNCTIONAL EXPENSES

Program services	72.1%	75.6%
Management and general	11.2%	11.7%
Fundraising	16.7%	12.7%
Total Expenses	100.0%	100.0% D

MIX OF REVENUE TYPES

Fundraising events revenue	24.8%	23.8%
Government grants	49.5%	51.8%
Contributions	24.5%	24.4%
In-kind contributions	1.2%	0.0%
Total Revenue and Support	100.0%	100.0% B

FUNDRAISING EFFECTIVENESS

Total Revenue	$ 5.86	$ 7.90
Total Revenue, less Government Grants	$ 2.96	$ 3.81 E

A : In 2015, All Good People (AGP) total revenue was $6,256,000. This was an increase of $266,000 from the prior year, a 4.4% improvement. This increase came from three areas: fundraising events ($125,000, an 8.8%, increase) and contributions and in-kind contributions ($75,000 increase each). There was a slight decrease in government grants of $9,000.

B : AGP's mix of revenue remained relatively stable. Government grants continue to be the largest component of revenue for AGP at 49.5% of total revenue. This was a slight decrease from 2014's 51.8%. Fundraising event revenue, on the other hand, increased to 24.8% of total revenue, a slight increase from 2014's 23.8%. Contributions remained relative flat at 24.5%, and in-kind contributions were new in 2015, at 1.2%. Here are my calculations for 2015:

$$\text{fundraising events} = \frac{1,550,000}{6,256,000} = 24.8\%$$

$$\text{government grants} = \frac{3,096,000}{6,256,000} = 49.5\%$$

$$\text{Contributions} = \frac{1,535,000}{6,256,000} = 24.5\%$$

$$\text{In-kind revenue} = \frac{75,000}{6,256,000} = 1.2\%$$

C: Total expenses for the organization also increased in 2015 to a total of $6,404,000, a $440,000 or 7.4% increase. Most of this increase was in the cost of fundraising. The costs of fundraising increased by $310,000 to a total of $1,068,000. Additionally, program expenses increased by $108,000 (2.4%) and management and administrative expenses increased by $22,000, or 3.2%.

D: Because of the significant additional fundraising expense, AGP saw a large increase, from 12.7% to 16.7%, of fundraising's share of total spending. Program services share of spending decreased from 75.6% to 72.1%, a negative trend that will need to be addressed in the current year. Management and general remained relatively flat at 11.2% in 2015. Here are my calculations for 2015:

$$\text{Program services} = \frac{4,619,000}{6,404,000} = 72.1\%$$

$$\text{Management \& General} = \frac{717,000}{6,404,000} = 11.2\%$$

$$\text{Fundraising} = \frac{1,068,000}{6,404,000} = 16.7\%$$

E: Because of the increased fundraising costs, the fundraising effectiveness measures decreased, both inclusive and exclusive of government grants. Based on total revenue, the fundraising department raised $5.86 per $ of fundraising cost in 2015. This is a significant decrease from $7.90 per $ in 2014. When excluding government grants, the ratio decreased to $2.96 from $3.81. Here are my calculations for 2015

$$\text{Total Revenue}: \frac{6,256,000}{1,068,000} = \$5.86$$

$$\text{Excluding government}: \frac{(6,256,000 - 3,096,000)}{1,068,000} = \$2.96$$

F: As a result of the 2015 performance, the net margin was negative 2.4%, largely due to the additional fundraising costs. This compares unfavorably to 2014 when the net margin was .4%. Here is my calculation for 2015

$$\text{Net margin} = \frac{-148,000}{6,256,000} = -2.4\%$$

Overall, the Statement of Activities for 2015 shows reasonably good performance with the exception of the cost of fundraising. The financial leader should require additional information to better understand the causes of the cost increase and how to address them in the current period.

Conclusion

The Income Statement is a summary of an organization's revenues and expenses for a specific period of time. When you apply certain analytical techniques and compare the results to a prior period, the power of the information becomes apparent, and the financial leader is enabled to ask questions or make decisions. While this statement is an effective report on the performance of the organization, it is not a statement about its overall health which we'll address in chapter 3. Our next statement, the Statement of Functional Expenses, will add some details to what we just covered in the expense section.

Here We Go...

CHAPTER

The Statement of Functional Expenses

Overview

After reviewing the Statement of Activities together in the previous chapter, we're ready for our next learning adventure. But first let's take a moment to review what we've already learned about our fictional organization, All Good People, Inc., from the Income Statement.

We can think of the Income Statement as giving us the view from 30,000 feet. At a high level, we now understand, in aggregate, how much revenue we received, how much in expenses we incurred, the amount of funds we were able to release from temporary restriction, and, critically, the change in net assets during the reporting period. We can also measure our progress by comparing the current period to the previous one.

But what if we want more detailed information about AGP's spending?

We know, for example, that AGP spent $717,000 on management and general expenses in the year ended June 30, 2015. But what exactly were those expenses? Is AGP spending in the right areas, or are there imbalances in the organization that should be addressed by management and the board?

To answer these questions, let's look at a statement that is closely related to the Income Statement—that is, the Statement of Functional Expenses. We can think of this second statement as a detailed report of the expenses section of the Income Statement. The Statement of Functional Expenses will give us the level of detail we need to make informed decisions about our spending priorities.

What Is It, What Is It Used For?

The Statement of Functional Expenses takes what we learned about expenses from the Income Statement, and allows us to drill down into each of the three high-level categories: program services, management and general, and fundraising. Here's a reminder of how these categories appear on the Income Statement.

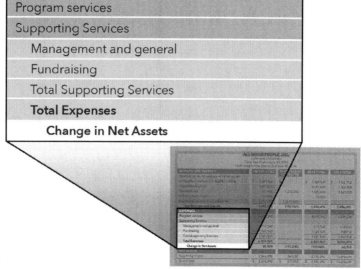

The Income Statement Has Gotten Us Only So Far

In order to fully understanding AGP's spending what we want to know now is: exactly what types of expenses are represented in each category? For example, in our analysis we noticed that expenses increased from the previous year. Was this because of an increase in salaries? Benefits? Professional fees? The Statement of Functional Expenses will help us instantly see where the changes are occurring. It will also let us compare spending across our functional areas in each particular period. So, pairing the Statement of Functional Expenses with the Income Statement, we will not only know the total expenses, but we will also know how much was spent on salaries, for instance. Or refreshments. Or insurance. There are many more expense types, so here we go.

Let's Break It Down

Let's return to All Good People, Inc. AGP's Statement of Functional Expenses for fiscal year ended June 30, 2015 is shown on the following page.

ALL GOOD PEOPLE, INC.

Statement of Functional Expenses

Fiscal Year Ended June 30, 2015

(with totals for the year ended June 30, 2014)

	Program Services	Management and General	Fundraising	Total Supporting Services	2015 Total	2014 Total
PERSONNEL						
Salaries	$ 2,659,000	$ 365,000	$ 567,000	$ 932,000	$ 3,591,000	$ 3,422,000
Employee benefits and payroll taxes	558,000	73,000	113,000	186,000	744,000	684,000
Total Personnel	3,217,000	438,000	680,000	1,118,000	4,335,000	4,106,000
Professional fees (includes in-kind legal fees of $75,000 in 2015)	358,000	186,000	82,000	268,000	626,000	490,000
Occupancy	71,000	12,000	16,000	28,000	99,000	102,000
Building and office supplies	91,000	4,000	21,000	25,000	116,000	105,000
Printing, publication and postage	71,000	5,000	55,000	60,000	131,000	94,000
Advertising	26,000		1,000	1,000	27,000	15,000
Program supplies	270,000		35,000	35,000	305,000	267,000
Food and refreshments	145,000	7,000	100,000	107,000	252,000	290,000
Equipment rental	22,000	2,000	4,000	6,000	28,000	21,000
Insurance	45,000	4,000	4,000	8,000	53,000	55,000
Repairs and maintenance	33,000	17,000	3,000	20,000	53,000	50,000
Interest	123,000	28,000	25,000	53,000	176,000	184,000
Depreciation	147,000	12,000	15,000	27,000	174,000	167,000
Bad debt			27,000	27,000	27,000	16,000
Bank fees		2,000		2,000	2,000	2,000
Total Other Expenses	1,402,000	279,000	388,000	667,000	2,069,000	1,858,000
	$ 4,619,000	$ 717,000	$ 1,068,000	$ 1,785,000	$ 6,404,000	$ 5,964,000

First, let's examine the title of the report, as well as the column headers.

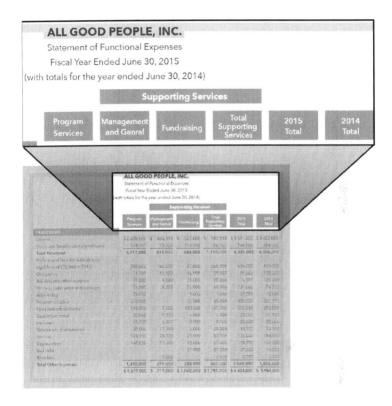

Similar to the Statement of Activities, the title of this second report includes the organization's name (All Good People, Inc.), the type of report (Statement of Functional Expenses), and the dates covered by the report (year ended June 30, 2015). Also like the Statement of Activities, the time period covered on the Statement of Functional Expenses is a *range of dates,* typically given as a month, quarter, or year. The date range will always match the one on the corresponding Statement of Activities. For our sample organization, we can see that the statement reflects activities for the fiscal year, ended June 30, 2015. For comparison purposes, it also shows the results for the prior year, June 30, 2014.

On the Income Statement, the functional expenses are organized in rows. There is an important difference on the Statement of Functional Expenses. Now, the functional expenses are organized in columns. This structure allows us to show the account-level detail for each specific function. You will notice that *program services* stands alone in its own column. The categories called *management and general* and *fundraising* have their own columns too, but they are also grouped together beneath the higher-level title *supporting services*. These groupings allow us to quickly reconcile totals between the Statement of Functional Expenses and Income Statement.

Let's Turn to the Contents of Each Row

As with the other financial statements, each row on the Statement of Functional Expenses relates to an *account*, or a group of associated accounts, in the organization's accounting system. By account, I mean a detailed financial category. The accounting system records transactions at the account level. The accounts are then grouped into broader, descriptive categories for reporting purposes. Here's an example: AGP may pay monthly rent for its facility, as well as water and electricity. Each of those could be accounts in the accounting system, and for reporting purposes they are combined into a category called occupancy.

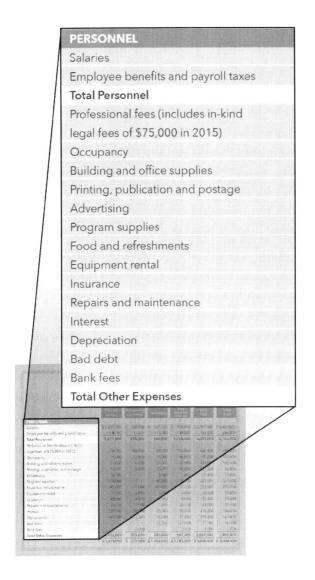

PERSONNEL

Salaries

Employee benefits and payroll taxes

Total Personnel

Professional fees (includes in-kind legal fees of $75,000 in 2015)

Occupancy

Building and office supplies

Printing, publication and postage

Advertising

Program supplies

Food and refreshments

Equipment rental

Insurance

Repairs and maintenance

Interest

Depreciation

Bad debt

Bank fees

Total Other Expenses

Don't be put off by the accounting language here; we are not learning to be accountants. What's important is that we can now see much more precisely how the organization has spent on each of its functions. As I said, this is critical information as you evaluate the effectiveness and efficiency of your spending.

What do Each of These Rows Mean?

I've shown in the above cutout for AGP one example of the categories of expenses a nonprofit might incur in a given year. Keep in mind that this particular list of expenditures is only one possibility, reflecting spending priorities at one fictitious organization. There can be any number of variations in these row titles, and the differences between them can be major or minor. The following representative list (with brief descriptions) will help broaden your vocabulary with regard to these types of expenses. It is not intended to be comprehensive, but it provides some key terms that financial leaders are likely to encounter and use.

Salaries is the row that contains salary and hourly wages paid to employees of the organization.

Employee Benefits and Payroll Taxes contains the additional costs for the organization to employ its staff, including for health care, retirement programs, and federal, state, and local taxes.

Professional fees are the costs of hiring third-party support and expertise. There are many reasons why an organization might require expertise that its internal staff cannot provide, and this row is where those expenses will be totaled.

Occupancy includes all facility costs, such as rent, electricity and gas.

Building and Office Supplies are everything from pens and paper to bathroom supplies and garbage bags.

Printing, Publication and Postage includes the cost of sending items to a third-party printer, and the cost of express or postal delivery services.

Advertising accounts for any money spent on promoting or marketing the organization's programs or events.

Program Supplies are generally the direct costs incurred by programmatic activities related to the organization's mission. This row can also include costs associated with specific fundraising activities.

Food and Refreshments, Equipment Rental, Insurance, Repairs and Maintenance, Interest, and **Bank Fees** are fairly well described by the titles themselves.

Depreciation is a method of spreading the cost of a non-current asset over its useful life. Examples are a building or certain office equipment. Depreciation is a non-cash expense, and will be discussed again when we get to the Statement of Cash Flows in chapter 4.

Bad Debt is an inevitable expense of any organization that has receivables on its Statement of Financial Position (discussed in the next chapter). This expense is the amount of receivables that have been declared not collectible.

What do the Numbers Mean, and How do they Relate?

The most important use of the Statement of Functional Expenses is the transparency it provides regarding organizational spending. The detailed listing of expense types, organized systematically by function, allows us to make reasoned judgments about spending priorities within and between years. To see this transparency in action, let's return to a question we asked earlier in relation to AGP: What caused the increase in fundraising expenses between the year ended June 30, 2014 and the year ended June 30, 2015? To answer the question, the finance leader now has an invaluable tool for making line-by-line comparisons in each functional category.

The Statement of Financial Position

(ALSO KNOWN AS THE BALANCE SHEET)

Overview

So far we have looked at two key statements for understanding revenues, expenses, and changes in net assets. Although the Income Statement and the Statement of Functional Expenses are essential to understanding your organization's financial performance, I want to use this chapter to look at the most important financial statement–the Statement of Financial Position, also known as the Balance Sheet.

The Balance Sheet is the most important financial statement because it provides cumulative, comprehensive financial information on your organization. Cumulative because it includes financial information from the organization's inception to the date of the report. And Comprehensive because it contains a complete record of the organization's assets and liabilities. Think of this as the report of your organizations overall health.

It is critical to understand the differences among these statements.

Recall the illustration on page 10, showing the interactions of the financial statements across time. We previously described both the Income Statement and the Statement of Functional Expenses as depicting the organization's performance over a specified period. The Balance Sheet is an accumulation, as of a specific date, of all of an organization's transactions since it began. Let's compare this concept to our own bodies. At the start of each year we evaluate ourselves physically, and make resolutions to correct what we don't like. Then, during the year, we live our lives, make good and bad decisions, exercise (or not), all the while affecting our bodies. At the end of the year we evaluate ourselves again to measure our changes. Here, the body is the Statement of Financial Position, beginning and ending every year. It is the cumulative result of activities and decisions since the day you were born. All those activities and decisions? These are like the financial details recorded in the statements of Activities and of Functional Expenses. These are the things an organization does. And on and on it goes, starting with a balance sheet, then making decisions and choices, and ending with a balance sheet. Every year offers up a new chance to improve in the next period.

What Is It, And What Is It Used For?

Recall that the Statement of Activities is "performance" related, showing what comes into and what goes out of the organization within a specific range of dates. In contrast, the Statement of Financial Position shows what an organization owns (assets) and owes (liabilities), and what is left over (net assets) of the assets after accounting for all obligations owed, at a specific point in time. The basic formula for the statement is as follows:

assets = liabilities + net assets

Let's Break It Down...

Below is the Balance Sheet for our fictional organization, AGP, Inc.

ALL GOOD PEOPLE, INC.
Statement of Financial Position
June 30, 2015
(with comparative amounts at June 30, 2014)

ASSETS	2015	2014
Cash and cash equivalents	$ 315,000	$ 418,000
Government grants receivables	678,000	851,000
Unconditional promises to give, net	516,000	468,000
Prepaid expenses and other assets	84,000	79,000
Current Assets	1,593,000	1,816,000
Property, plant and equipment, net	2,726,000	2,900,000
	$ 4,319,000	$ 4,716,000

LIABILITIES AND NET ASSETS	2015	2014
Liabilities		
Accounts payable and accrued expenses	$ 184,000	$ 368,000
Accrued salaries	22,000	18,000
Accrued vacation	95,000	93,000
Current Liabilities	301,000	479,000
Mortgage payable	1,136,000	1,207,000
Total Liabilities	1,437,000	1,686,000
Net Assets		
Unrestricted	2,605,000	2,566,000
Temporarily restricted	277,000	464,000
Total Net Assets	2,882,000	3,030,000
	$ 4,319,000	$ 4,716,000

First, let's examine the title of the report, and column headers.

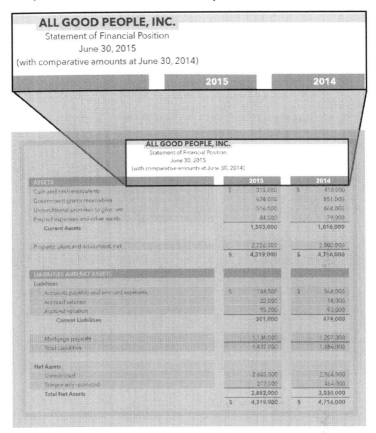

ALL GOOD PEOPLE, INC.
Statement of Financial Position
June 30, 2015
(with comparative amounts at June 30, 2014)

	2015	2014
ASSETS		
Cash and cash equivalents	$ 315,000	$ 418,000
Government grants receivables	678,000	851,000
Unconditional promises to give, net	516,000	468,000
Prepaid expenses and other assets	84,000	79,000
Current Assets	1,593,000	1,816,000
Property, plant and equipment, net	2,726,000	2,900,000
	$ 4,319,000	$ 4,716,000
LIABILITIES AND NET ASSETS		
Liabilities		
Accounts payable and accrued expenses	$ 184,000	$ 368,000
Accrued salaries	22,000	18,000
Accrued vacation	95,000	93,000
Current Liabilities	301,000	479,000
Mortgage payable	1,136,000	1,207,000
Total Liabilities	1,437,000	1,686,000
Net Assets		
Unrestricted	2,605,000	2,566,000
Temporarily restricted	277,000	464,000
Total Net Assets	2,882,000	3,030,000
	$ 4,319,000	$ 4,716,000

As we've seen on the previous two statements, the title of the report includes the organization's name (All Good People, Inc.), the type of report (here, the Statement of Financial Position), and the date of the report (June 30, 2015). To repeat, the time period for the Balance Sheet is not a range of dates, but a specific "as of" date, typically a month-end, quarter-end, or year-end. For AGP, we can see that the statement reflects balances as of the last day of the fiscal year, June 30, 2015. It also shows the results as of the last day of the prior year, June 30, 2014, for comparison purposes.

The Rows

The rows display the Balance Sheet equation in its three main sections: **Assets, Liabilities**, and **Net Assets**. Assets are what is owned by the organization, liabilities are amounts owed, and net assets are simply assets minus liabilities.

What Is an Asset?

An asset is something that the organization owns or is owed. Assets are typically listed in order of *liquidity*, or nearness to cash. Cash is therefore always listed first. There are two main categories of assets: current and non-current. Current assets are expected to be used within one year, and non-current assets are expected to last longer than one year. Keeping clear on this distinction adds important analytical value to the Balance Sheet, as we will see later in the chapter.

Let's Take a Look at Some Assets.

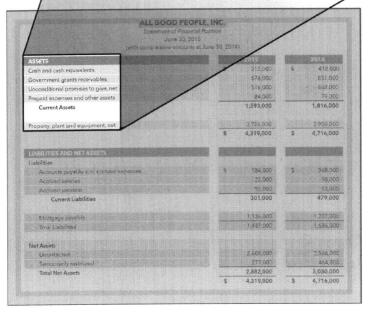

ASSETS

Cash and cash equivalents

Government grants receivables

Unconditional promises to give, net

Prepaid expenses and other assets

Current Assets

Property, plant and equipment, net

ALL GOOD PEOPLE, INC.
Statement of Financial Position
June 30, 2015
(with comparative amounts at June 30, 2014)

ASSETS	2015	2014
Cash and cash equivalents	919,000	$ 418,000
Government grants receivables	578,000	651,000
Unconditional promises to give, net	516,000	668,000
Prepaid expenses and other assets	84,000	79,000
Current Assets	1,593,000	1,816,000
Property, plant and equipment, net	2,726,000	2,900,000
	$ 4,319,000	$ 4,716,000

LIABILITIES AND NET ASSETS	2015	2014
Liabilities		
Accounts payable and accrued expenses	$ 184,000	$ 368,000
Accrued salaries	22,000	18,000
Accrued vacation	95,000	93,000
Current Liabilities	301,000	479,000
Mortgage payable	1,136,000	1,207,000
Total Liabilities	1,437,000	1,686,000
Net Assets		
Unrestricted	2,605,000	2,566,000
Temporarily restricted	277,000	464,000
Total Net Assets	2,882,000	3,030,000
	$ 4,319,000	$ 4,716,000

Cash (or cash and cash equivalents) consists of cash balances in checking and savings accounts, as well as any additional cash kept in a petty cash fund. *Cash* is immediately available for use.

Receivables are typically money owed to the organization in return for goods or services provided, or as a result of a contractual obligation such as a government grant. This is simply an example from our sample statement. In practice, you may see other types of receivables, like Medicaid or insurance payments receivable.

Unconditional Promises to give are donor gifts that have been promised to the organization but not yet collected. This type of asset is very similar to receivables, although there are technical differences between receivables and unconditional promises to give. A receivable is typically money owed to the organization in return for goods or services provided. Unconditional promises to give are monies promised to the organization, but by donors, where there has been no exchange of goods or services.

Prepaid Expenses are expenses required to be paid up front, however, they cover a future period of time. An example of this type of expense is insurance, which often must be paid a year in advance. It qualifies as an asset because, once paid for, it is something owned by the organization. This asset amount is decreased each month as insurance is "used."

Property, Plant and Equipment (non-current) are the hard assets an organization invests in or purchases with the expectation that these assets will last for a long period of time. Examples are buildings, vehicles, or certain office equipment.

What Are Liabilities?

Liabilities are the amounts owed by the organization, typically listed by how soon the amounts need to be repaid. As with the assets section, liabilities are also segregated into current and non-current categories. Current liabilities are obligations due within one year. I mentioned the analytical importance of the distinction between current and non-current. Keeping this distinction in mind, we will soon investigate the relationship between current assets and current liabilities.

Let's First Define Various Types of Liabilities.

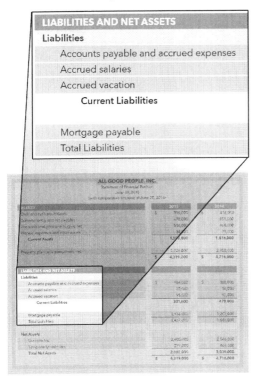

Accounts Payable are amounts owed to vendors of the organization, for which invoices have been received and entered into the accounting system. These amounts will typically be paid within thirty days.

Accrued Expenses are amounts due to be paid within one year, for which services or products have been received but no invoice has yet been submitted. These can include amounts owed to vendors, but are more likely to be amounts owed to employees, like **accrued salaries** or **accrued vacation**.

Some organizations may own their facilities and have mortgages or other long-term debt obligation outstanding. These obligations might have names such as "mortgage" or "note payable." In the liabilities section of the statement they would be classified as *non-current*, because they are expected to last longer than one year.

What Are Net Assets?

Technically, net assets shows the cumulative amount that remains after subtracting liabilities from assets. This can be thought of as the organization's *net worth*, the accumulated value of the organization since inception. Over time, as net assets increase, the overall stability and fiscal sustainability of the organization are also increasing.

Net Assets
Unrestricted
Temporarily restricted
Total Net Assets

ALL GOOD PEOPLE, INC.
Statement of Financial Position
June 30, 2015
(with comparative amounts at June 30, 2014)

ASSETS		2015		2014
Cash and cash equivalents	$	315,000	$	418,000
Government grants receivables		678,000		851,000
Unconditional promises to give, net		515,000		468,000
Prepaid expenses and other assets		84,000		79,000
Current Assets		1,595,000		1,816,000
Property, plant and equipment, net		2,726,000		2,900,000
	$	4,319,000	$	4,716,000
LIABILITIES AND NET ASSETS				
Liabilities				
Accounts payable and accrued expenses	$	184,000	$	368,000
Accrued salaries		22,000		18,000
Accrued vacation		95,000		93,000
Current Liabilities		301,000		479,000
Mortgage payable		1,136,000		1,207,000
Total Liabilities		1,437,000		1,686,000
Net Assets				
Unrestricted		2,605,000		2,566,000
Temporarily restricted		277,000		464,000
Total Net Assets		2,882,000		3,030,000
	$	4,319,000	$	4,716,000

You will see that net assets balances are categorized by restriction type: unrestricted and temporarily restricted. In many cases you will also encounter a category called permanently restricted. There are two important things to note here.

First, net assets are the residual value of the organization. But that is only part of the story. To ensure prudent planning, we must also know how much of that value is available to management and the board (unrestricted), as opposed to how much is still restricted by ongoing obligations to the wishes of the respective donors (temporarily and permanently restricted).

Second, net assets is where the Income Statement links to the Balance Sheet. Remember where we showed *change in net assets* for each column of the Statement of Activities? That change is the difference between the net assets balances. This is true every time the financial statements are issued. The change in net assets on the Income Statement will equal the difference between net asset balances on the Balance Sheet.

What do the Numbers Mean, and How Do They Relate to Each Other?

Take a look again at our example Statement of Financial Position. Note that there are two columns of financial information, one for the current year and one for the prior year. Let's walk through the statement, thinking about how best to approach and utilize the information.

How Much Cash Is There?

The first place most folks look on the Statement of Financial Position is at *cash*. How much cash do we have? This is a great question, but simply looking at the balance doesn't help us understand whether the balance is sufficient or not. The following simple calculations help a financial leader understand the organization's adequacy of cash.

Measuring Liquidity

Current ratio - As mentioned previously, the Balance Sheet has "current" totals for both assets and liabilities. Current is defined as those assets to be used, or debts to be paid, within one year. In other words, this relationship measures the organization's ability to meet its current obligations with current assets. The formula for the current ratio is below. The desirable result is typically greater than 1.0, indicating that current assets are more than adequate to pay current liabilities. The higher the number, the better.

$$current\ ratio = \frac{current\ assets}{currenet\ liabilities}$$

Quick ratio - Similar to the current ratio, the quick ratio assesses the organization's ability to meet its short-term debt obligations with only its most liquid assets. I suggest using the cash balance for this ratio. Once again, a larger result is better.

$$quick\ ratio = \frac{cash\ and\ cash\ equivalents}{current\ liabilities}$$

Days of cash on hand - When we think about having adequate cash, one of the best ways to measure is to compare available cash to average (or typical) cash expenses. Again, a higher number of days is better.

$$days\ of\ cash\ on\ hand = \frac{cash\ and\ cash\ equivalents}{total\ annual\ expenses - depreciation} *365\ days$$

Days to collect receivables - Receivables represent the

amounts owed to your organization. It is critical to manage receivables, as they are far more useful to an organization once they have been converted to cash. One way to measure the organization's effectiveness at managing receivables is to calculate the average number of days to collect. This can be done for each type of revenue, as long as the required information is provided. Note that, in this case, lower numbers are better.

The first formula looks at all amounts owed to your organization, including government grants receivable and unconditional promises to give, both found on the Statement of Financial Position. These amounts are compared to the total revenues generated during the year, found on the Statement of Activities, in the row titled "Total Revenue and Support."

$$days\ to\ collect\ receivables, total = \frac{total\ receivables}{total\ revenue} * 365\ days$$

The second formula is more specific. In it we are only looking at the amount of time it takes for an organization to collect what it is owed by government agencies. So we only use the government receivables (from the Statement of Financial Position) and government grant revenue (from the Statement of Activities) for this calculation.

$$days\ to\ collect\ receivables, govt. = \frac{total\ govt.\ receivables}{total\ govt.\ revenue} * 365\ days$$

We can similarly focus only on the unconditional promises to give, using that amount from the Statement of Financial Position, and contribution revenue from the Statement of Activities.

$$\text{days to collect receivables, unconditional promises} = \frac{\text{total uncond. promises to give}}{\text{total contribution revenue}} *365 \text{ days}$$

These ratios can tell a lot about management's style, as well as its financial (and fundraising) competencies. Different ratio values can trigger important questions for an organization's leaders. If it takes three to four months to receive reimbursement for government grants, is there a problem with the invoices the organization is sending? Does the government agency struggle with understanding the supporting documents the organization provides? Similarly, why would it take a very long time to coordinate payments from donors? Is there a problem with sending statements, or with the information in internal systems? Are there certain donors that management would rather not pester for payment? Each of these questions is important to the financial leader. The longer it takes to collect receivables, the more money needs to be raised to fund the outstanding amounts.

Measuring the Unrestricted Reserve - Unrestricted Reserve is the amount the organization has accumulated for uncommitted spending, like a rainy day fund or a fund for new programming. Think of this as a savings account that can be used as agreed by management and the board. Here's the formula:

$$\textit{unrestricted reserve} = \textit{unrestricted net assets} - \textit{noncurrent assets}$$

Organizations that have made significant investments in non-current assets (such as a building) may find the unrestricted reserve very low, or even negative. This means the organization has limited or no liquid reserves, as they are tied up in the long-term assets.

Measuring debt - It's critical for financial leaders to be mindful of accumulating debt. The debt-to-equity ratio is a useful measure here. This ratio tells us how much debt (versus assets) is being used to support the organization. The calculation is:

$$\textit{debt to equity} = \frac{\textit{total liabilities}}{\textit{total net assets}}$$

In some cases, especially when there is a significant balance of restricted net assets, a financial leader may use "unrestricted net assets" in the denominator, as these are the net assets most likely to be used to pay down the liabilities.

Each of these ratios can be calculated for prior periods (or for the budget), and the results can be compared to the current year. Just like we did with the Income Statement, this is the horizontal analysis, meaning we are analyzing items across each row. When compared to each other, the results provide powerful tools that can help the financial leader ask appropriate questions about management of financial results.

You can also simply subtract the current Balance Sheet

data from prior periods. For example, in 2014 our ending cash balance was $418,000 and in 2015 it was $315,000. By subtracting the current amount from the previous amount, we can see that the cash balance decreased by $103,000. And, just as we did with the Income Statement, we can calculate variances in both dollars and percentages from previous periods or budgets. Again using the cash example described previously, cash decreased during the year by $103,000, from $418,000, a 24.6% decrease in cash. These calculations provide perspective and help the financial leader ask key questions regarding changes based on where the organization was, or where it had planned to be.

Building a Narrative

Next, you can review the narrative I've written based on the sample Statement of Financial Position presented in this chapter. Our fictitious organization, All Good People, has just completed its annual audit. As a financial leader it is your responsibility to explain the resulting Statement of Financial Position to an audience, such as board members, who are not always experts in financial reporting.

Now, using the Statement of Financial Position shown previously, we will make comparisons to the prior year and apply all of the calculations we just discussed. In this way, along with my added narrative, you can see how I use the results to describe AGP's fiscal health.

ALL GOOD PEOPLE, INC.

Statement of Financial Position

June 30, 2015

(with comparative amounts at June 30, 2014)

	2015	2014	2015 vs. 2014
ASSETS			
Cash and cash equivalents	$ 315,000	$ 418,000	$ (103,000)
Government grants receivable	678,000	851,000	(173,000)
Unconditional promises to give, net	516,000	468,000	48,000
Prepaid expenses and other assets	84,000	79,000	5,000
Current Assets	1,593,000	1,816,000	(223,000)
Property, plant and equipment, net	2,726,000	2,900,000	(174,000)
	$ 4,319,000	**$ 4,716,000**	**$ (397,000)**
LIABILITIES AND NET ASSETS			
Liabilities			
Accounts payable and accrued expenses	$ 184,000	$ 368,000	$ (184,000)
Accrued salaries	22,000	18,000	4,000
Accrued vacation	95,000	93,000	2,000
Current Liabilities	301,000	479,000	(178,000)
Mortgage payable	1,136,000	1,207,000	(71,000)

A

B

	C	E	G
Total Liabilities	(249,000)	1,686,000	1,437,000
Net Assets			
Unrestricted	39,000	2,566,000	2,605,000
Temporarily restricted	(187,000)	464,000	277,000
Total Net Assets	(148,000)	3,030,000	2,882,000
	$ (397,000)	$ 4,716,000	$ 4,319,000
Current Ratio	1.50	3.79	5.29
Quick Ratio	0.18	0.87	1.05
Days of Cash on Hand	(7.8)	26.3	18.5
Days to Collect Receivables			
Total Receivables	9.9	80.4	70.5
Government Contracts	20.1	100.0	79.9
Unconditional promises to give, net	(1.9)	59.2	61.1
Operating (Unrestricted) Reserve	13.9	(21.0)	(7.1)
Debt to-Net Assets (or Debt-to-Equity)	0.06	0.56	0.50

D

F

H

A Total assets decreased from the previous year by $397,000. The largest portion of this decrease was from regularly occurring depreciation expense of the property, plant and equipment. In addition, both cash and government grants receivable decreased, by $103,000 and $173,000 respectively.

B Total liabilities decreased by $249,000, driven by a large pay-down of accounts payable, which decreased by $184,000. This is the likely explanation of the decrease of cash noted above. In addition, the organization made monthly mortgage payments resulting in a $71,000 decrease of its outstanding mortgage balance.

C Unrestricted net assets increased slightly (by $39,000), while temporarily restricted net assets decreased by $187,000.

D In analyzing the organization's liquidity, we can see that the current ratio increased from 3.79 to 5.29. This improvement was driven by the substantial decrease in current liabilities. The quick ratio increased modestly, from 0.87 to 1.05, indicating that the organization has enough cash to pay its current liabilities in total, as of the date of the report.

$$\text{Current ratio} = \frac{1,593,000}{301,000} = 5.29$$

$$\text{Quick ratio} = \frac{315,000}{301,000} = 1.05$$

E Days of cash on hand decreased from over 26 days to 18.5 days, caused largely by the significant payment of accounts payable.

$$\text{Days Cash on hand} = \frac{315,000}{(6,404,000 - 174,000)} \times 365 = 18.5 \text{ days}$$

F Days to collect receivables decreased from the previous year, a positive indicator that the organization is improving its ability to efficiently convert receivables to cash. In total, the number of days to collect all receivables improved from over 80 days to just over 70 days. The primary driver of this improvement was a large improvement in collection of outstanding government grants. In the previous year, the organization had 100 days of government receivables, while this year that improved to just better than 80.

$$\text{Total} = \frac{(678,000 + 516,000)}{(1,550,000 + 3,094,000 + 1,535,000)} \times 365 = 70.5 \text{ days}$$

$$\text{government} = \frac{678,000}{3,094,000} \times 365 = 79.9 \text{ days}$$

$$\text{Promises to give} = \frac{516,000}{(1,550,000 + 1,535,000)} \times 365 = 61.1 \text{ days}$$

G The organization's operating reserve, while still negative, improved from -21 days to -7 days. While this number should be positive, the organization made a healthy improvement in this measure. The organization is moving away from using its property, plant and equipment as its reserve.

$$\text{Days of operating reserve} = \frac{(2,605,000 - 2,774,000)}{(6,404,000 - 174,000)} \times 365 = -7.1 \text{ days}$$

HThe organization continues to improve its debt-to-equity as it makes regular payment against its outstanding mortgage balance. Last year, the ratio was 0.56, and it improved to 0.50, indicating less reliance upon debt for supporting the organization.

$$\text{Debt - to - net assets} = \frac{1,437,000}{2,882,000} = .50$$

Conclusion

The Balance Sheet is a cumulative, comprehensive display of an organization's financial health from its inception to a specified date. It is the statement that depicts the overall health of the organization. We have learned a number of techniques and ratios that, when applied to the data found on a Balance Sheet, can provide a powerful basis for the financial leader to identify important questions, challenge practices, and make informed decisions.

We have now covered three of the four main financial statements. Take a deep breath, then let's get to work on the last one—the Statement of Cash Flows.

CHAPTER

The Statement of Cash Flows

Overview

Our fourth and final key financial report is **the Statement of Cash Flows.** This important financial statement tells you about the changes in your cash balance, which is critical for your organization. But I'll be straight forward with you. The Statement of Cash Flows is probably the most confusing to prepare and to read. The good news is that we're not going to learn how to *prepare* this statement in this chapter. Your finance staff will prepare it. This chapter is about how you, as a financial leader, should read, interpret, and use it in your decision-making. Our mission is to learn to use the information provided. Let's turn to the key parts of the statement.

What is it, What is it Used For?

Cash is the lifeblood of the organization, so we need to have a regularly reported way to measure the inflows (sources) and outflows (uses) of the organization's cash. So far we've talked about revenue, expenses, and income. But we have never tried to relate these terms to cash. That's the purpose of the cash flow statement.

The reason we can't just "run a cash report" is because of accrual accounting. Most organizations today use accrual (or modified accrual) accounting. This means that many activities are recorded in the accounting system that have no impact on cash. For example: A donor pledges $10,000 to your organization. This is great news! It's entered into the accounting system as a "pledge" (not cash), there is no bank deposit. Your organization's Statement of Activities for that period will show the $10,000 but it will be classified as an unconditional promises to give. We show the pledge as revenue, but, very importantly, not as cash.

Here's another example: You receive the previous month's electric bill, but you delay payment so no cash has left your bank account. How should we account for this obligation? Here, your organization will record the unpaid bill as an expense on the Statement of Activities and a liability (accounts payable) on the Statement of Financial Position. But it does not affect your cash position.

These are only two of the many types of non-cash accrual transactions that can be entered into the accounting system during any given month. The purpose of the Statement of Cash Flows is to recognize and adjust for all those non-cash entries. As I said, the process of preparing the Statement of Cash Flows is rather complicated but that's the accountant's job. For now, it is important to see that the Statement of Cash Flows shows the organization's activity as if only cash transactions occurred. There are also a few critical data points on the statement to help the financial leader.

Let's Break it Down

Below is the Statement of Cash Flows for AGP, Inc. for their fiscal year ended June 30, 2015.

ALL GOOD P[

Statement of
Fiscal Year Ende[
(with totals for the year

CASH FLOWS FROM OPERATING ACTIVITIES

Change in net assets

Adjustments to reconcile change in net assets to net cash from operating activities

Depreciation

Changes in operating assets and liabilities

Government grants receivable

Unconditional promises to give

Prepaid expenses

Accounts payable and accrued expenses

Net Cash from Operating Activities

CASH FLOWS FROM INVESTING ACTIVITIES

Purchase of property, plant and equipment

CASH FLOWS FROM FINANCING ACTIVITIES

Principal payments on loans

Net Change in Cash and Cash Equivalents

CASH AND CASH EQUIVALENTS

Beginning of year

End of year

EOPLE, INC.

Cash Flows
June 30, 2015
ended June 30, 2014)

	2015	2014
$	(148,000)	$ 26,000
	174,000	167,000
	173,000	(66,000)
	(48,000)	37,000
	(5,000)	6,000
	(178,000)	86,000
	(32,000)	256,000
		(74,000)
	(71,000)	(60,000)
	(103,000)	122,000
	418,000	296,000
$	315,000	$ 418,000

First, let's examine the title of the report, as well as the column headers

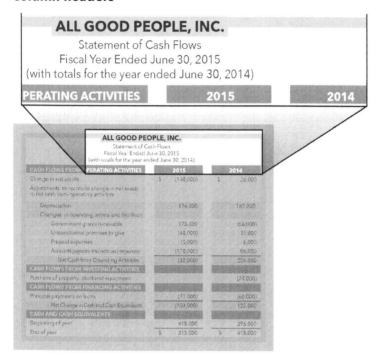

ALL GOOD PEOPLE, INC.
Statement of Cash Flows
Fiscal Year Ended June 30, 2015
(with totals for the year ended June 30, 2014)

PERATING ACTIVITIES	2015	2014

ALL GOOD PEOPLE, INC. Statement of Cash Flows Fiscal Year Ended June 30, 2015 (with totals for the year ended June 30, 2014)		
CASH FLOWS FROM OPERATING ACTIVITIES	2015	2014
Change in net assets	$ (148,000)	$ 26,000
Adjustments to reconcile change in net assets to net cash from operating activities		
Depreciation	174,000	167,000
Changes in operating assets and liabilities		
Government grants receivable	173,000	(66,000)
Unconditional promises to give	(48,000)	37,000
Prepaid expenses	(5,000)	6,000
Accounts payable and accrued expenses	(178,000)	66,000
Net Cash from Operating Activities	(32,000)	256,000
CASH FLOWS FROM INVESTING ACTIVITIES		
Purchase of property, plant and equipment		(74,000)
CASH FLOWS FROM FINANCING ACTIVITIES		
Principal payments on loans	(71,000)	(60,000)
Net Change in Cash and Cash Equivalents	(103,000)	122,000
CASH AND CASH EQUIVALENTS		
Beginning of year	418,000	296,000
End of year	$ 315,000	$ 418,000

The title of the report includes the organization's name (All Good People, Inc.), the type of report (Statement of Cash Flows), and the dates covered by the report (year ended June 30, 2015). As with the Income Statement and the Statement of Functional Expenses, the time period for the Statement of Cash Flows is a range of dates, typically a month, quarter, or year. For our sample organization, we can see that the statement reflects activities for the fiscal year, ended June 30, 2015. For comparison purposes, it also shows the results for the prior year, June 30, 2014.

The Rows

The statement is structured in three main categories: operating, investing, and financing activities.

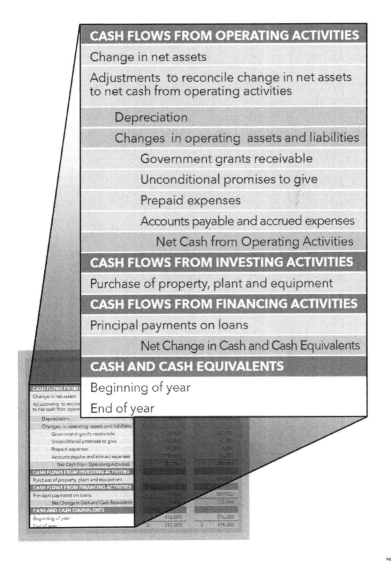

CASH FLOWS FROM OPERATING ACTIVITIES
Change in net assets
Adjustments to reconcile change in net assets to net cash from operating activities
Depreciation
Changes in operating assets and liabilities
Government grants receivable
Unconditional promises to give
Prepaid expenses
Accounts payable and accrued expenses
Net Cash from Operating Activities
CASH FLOWS FROM INVESTING ACTIVITIES
Purchase of property, plant and equipment
CASH FLOWS FROM FINANCING ACTIVITIES
Principal payments on loans
Net Change in Cash and Cash Equivalents
CASH AND CASH EQUIVALENTS
Beginning of year
End of year

Operating Activities are the core activities of your organization. As a consequence, they should provide the bulk of its cash flows. The logic behind this section is that we begin with your change in net assets (from the Income Statement), and then adjust it to account for all accrual transactions. The result of this calculation is cash flows from operating activities. This is an extremely meaningful number, since you will almost always expect it to be positive. A negative number here will need to be very well understood, and actions taken to remedy the situation.

Investing Activities occur when your organization purchases or sells assets. The cash impact of those changes will show up in this section. In order to spend money on new assets, the organization must either have generated cash from operating activities, or have received cash from taking out a loan (recorded in the financing section). These are the only ways for organizations to purchase assets. As with the operating section, the key information in this section is the total—that is, sum of all cash from investing activities.

Financing Activities is the last category. If your organization has debt, loans, or a mortgage, the cash impact of these transactions will appear here. As with the previous sections, the total—that is, the sum of all cash from financing activities— is the important measure in this section.

Finally, at the end of the statement we see cash and cash equivalents. This is also, importantly, where we find a linkage between the Statement of Cash Flows and the Statement of Financial Position. The financial leader can now see two key features of the statement: first, how the net change in cash and cash equivalents over the current period affects the cash balance, and, second, how this number also matches the balances on the Balance Sheet.

What do the numbers mean, and how do they relate to each other?

Take a look at the current period, and think through the following questions.

How much cash has the organization created (positive number) or used (negative number)? Did the organization produce positive cash flow during the period? If so, was the positive cash flow from operating activities? If not, the organization must have sold assets (investing activities) or taken out a loan (financing activities) to reach an overall positive amount.

How much cash did the organization spend servicing debt or buying assets? If the organization has debt, can you see how much cash is required to service that debt for the current and prior periods?

ALL GOOD

Statement
Fiscal Year End
(with totals for the yea

CASH FLOWS FROM OPERATING ACTIVITIES	
Change in net assets	$
Adjustments to reconcile change in net assets	
to net cash from operating activities	
Depreciation	
Changes in operating assets and liabilities	
Government grants receivable	
Unconditional promises to give	
Prepaid expenses	
Accounts payable and accrued expenses	
Net Cash from Operating Activities	
CASH FLOWS FROM INVESTING ACTIVITIES	
Purchase of property, plant and equipment	
CASH FLOWS FROM FINANCING ACTIVITIES	
Principal payments on loans	
Net Change in Cash and Cash Equivalents	
CASH AND CASH EQUIVALENTS	**D**
Beginning of year	
End of year	$

Building a Narrative

Below is a sample narrative based on the Statement of
Cash Flows for All Good People, Inc. As with the earlier
statements, it is your responsibility, as a financial leader, to

of Cash Flows
ded June 30, 2015
ar ended June 30, 2014)

2015	2014	2015 vs. 2014	
(148,000)	$ 26,000		
174,000	167,000		**A**
173,000	(66,000)		
(48,000)	37,000		
(5,000)	6,000		
(178,000)	86,000		
(32,000)	256,000	(288,000)	
	(74,000)	74,000	**B**
			C
(71,000)	(60,000)	(11,000)	
(103,000)	122,000	(225,000)	
418,000	296,000		
315,000	$ 418,000		

understand what the Statement of Cash Flows is telling you and to explain it to your board or other key stakeholders. The following assessment of the organization's results will give you an example of how to do it.

A Cash flows from operating activities decreased substantially from the prior year, from $256,000 to a negative $32,000, a total decrease of $288,000. For the current year, although change in net assets was a loss of $148,000 (based on accrual accounting), the organization actually lost $32,000 in cash.

B The organization acquired no assets in the current year, compared to $74,000 of asset purchases the prior year. This results in a positive variance of $74,000.

C The organization has a mortgage that required $71,000 of principal payments during the current year, $11,000 more than the prior year.

In total, the organization used $225,000 more cash than the prior year.

D The organization started the current year with $418,000 in cash, and it used $103,000 during the year. This left AGP with $315,000 cash at the end of the current period, which is also shown at the top of the Statement of Financial Position.

More on Some Additional Key Topics

The Audited Financial Statements

When we began our work together, we laid out the four primary financial statements that you will encounter as a nonprofit financial leader. I recommended early on that you keep your organization's audited statements within reach as we worked our way through the statements. What you may have noticed is that there is more to this set of statements than just the four we have discussed so far.

To complete our understanding, let's discuss two additional, accompanying reports important to your nonprofit's financial health: the auditor's opinion letter, and the notes to the financial statements.

Auditor's Opinion Letter

On an annual basis your organization is audited to ensure its financial statements are "fairly presented." Although the audit process is quite detailed, auditors are not certifying the financial statements for accuracy. It is their role to perform tests that enable them to provide an overall opinion as to the reasonableness of your financial statements and internal controls.

The best result you can expect is what is called an *unqualified* opinion. This means the financials are fairly presented in accordance with generally accepted accounting principles (GAAP).

You may also receive (but hopefully will not) a *qualified* opinion. This is generally the same as unqualified, except that the auditors found a single instance of noncompliance with GAAP, or they experienced some type of *scope limitation* while performing the audit. Such a limitation can occur, for example, when there is a loss of data or backup materials.

Finally, the most negative result is an *adverse* opinion. This occurs when the financial statements are found to be materially misstated. In other words, the information is incorrect, unreliable, or inaccurate.

As a financial leader, your goal for the accounting team is always an unqualified opinion. And yes, this matters a lot to donors. When asked to give, your organization's benefactors must be assured that your organization has the skills and knowledge to account correctly for their donations. To ensure your organization is observing best practices, you should identify the most recent opinion of the auditors. If it is anything other than unqualified, ask what is being done at present to mitigate the issue. This should be done without hesitation, but certainly prior to the end of the subsequent fiscal year.

Example Unqualified Opinion

In our opinion, the financial statements referred to above **present fairly, in all material respects**, the financial position of All Good People, Inc. as of December 31, 20XX, and the results of its operations and its cash flows for the year then ended in accordance with accounting principles generally accepted in the United States of America.

Example Qualified Opinion

In our opinion, **except for the effects of** <the GAAP compliance or scope limitation is described here> as discussed in the preceding paragraph, the financial statements referred to above present fairly, in all material respects, the financial position of All Good People, Inc. as of December 31, 20XX, and the results of its operations and its cash flows for the year then ended in accordance with accounting principles generally accepted in the United States of America.

Example Adverse Opinion

In our opinion, because of the effects of the matters discussed in the preceding paragraphs, the financial statements referred to above **do not present fairly**, in accordance with accounting principles generally accepted in the United States of America, the financial position of All Good People, Inc. as of December 31, 20XX, or the results of its operations or its cash flows for the year then ended.

Notes to the Financial Statements

Have you ever been told to read the fine print? For the four financial statements we've reviewed, the notes to the financial statements are the fine print. They include a substantial amount of detail critical to further understanding the financial information in the statements themselves. The notes provide information about the organization, its purpose, and its activities. This is followed by a detailed explanation of accounting policies used to develop the financial statements. Finally, there are additional sections including detailed schedules of items such as long-term debt payment schedules, pension plans, and long-term assets.

Deeper Exploration of Other Concepts

As we have progressed through the four statements, we have touched on some critical areas of knowledge. I promised at the outset I would not try to teach you accounting, and I have tried to keep my explanations pithy. Below I have identified a few of the areas and concepts in need of further expansion, and have described them more fully.

Restrictions

We briefly discussed restrictions when we covered the Statement of Activities in chapter 1. Since this concept is critical to the proper functioning and reporting of nonprofit finances, we should dig a little deeper. Some of this has been covered previously, but since it is important information I have included it again here.

Donors have the ability to impose restrictions on gifts made to an organization. These restrictions come in two categories: purpose restrictions and time restrictions. A purpose restriction limits the use of a gift to a specific activity, while a time restriction limits the use of the gift to a certain period of time. They are known as temporarily restricted donations, since both types of restriction can ultimately be satisfied. Once satisfied, the temporary restriction is released, and the funds become unrestricted. We saw how this situation is portrayed on the Statement of Activities.

Donors also have the ability to restrict donations permanently. A permanently restricted gift will typically come with instructions for investing the funds, a condition that the principal amount remains in perpetuity, and guidance for the use of earnings generated by the principal.

Accounting guidelines require that restricted gifts be recognized in the organization's financial statements in the period in which they are received, not the period in which they are used. This is the main reason the Income Statement is arranged in its columnar format, without which it would be easy to mistake restricted for unrestricted donations. Confusion between restricted and unrestricted funds is bad for the donor and bad for the organization. As a financial leader, when you demand the columnar format on the Income Statement, you are sending the message that you take donor-imposed restrictions very seriously.

Accrual Accounting Versus Cash Basis Accounting

I am asked frequently: Why do we use accrual accounting, then go to all the trouble of generating a cash flow statement? Can't we just do our accounting in cash? Well, no.

Cash basis accounting is simple. In this type of accounting, we only record transactions that affect cash. If a donor drops by the office with cash or a check, we will record that as a gift on the date received, and the development department scores a win. If a donor emails a promise to give, and says she will pay if we send a statement, there is no gift in cash basis accounting. Development does not get to record this as a win. (Yet.)

With accrual accounting, however, we record all transactions regardless of their cash impact. For example, we would record the emailed pledge (or promise to give) as a current month gift, and we would have a balance in unconditional promises to give.

By definition, accrual accounting creates the notions of accounts receivable and accounts payable. Accrual accounting is more accurate because it captures and recognizes all transactions, which is why most organizations are required to utilize it.

Direct Versus Indirect Expenses

Although many expenses can be clearly categorized as either direct (program) or indirect (management, administrative, or fundraising), many cannot. What is the clarification process, and how does it work?

First, we should re-examine why this distinction is important. Most donors want their gifts to be applied to services that directly further the mission of the organization. This is certainly the case with restricted gifts and government grants. As an example, consider the coach of an after school program. The coach's payroll costs are clearly a direct cost. Additionally, that coach has a desk, a computer, and phone, and uses other office services as well. These are examples of indirect costs. So the total costs for the coach include the payroll costs (direct) and the office costs (indirect). If restricted or government grant fund cover only her direct costs, then the indirect costs must be covered by unrestricted funds.

Applying this distinction between direct and indirect costs is done through an accounting process called allocations. Various indirect costs are allocated to most accurately reflect the total cost of providing a program. The allocation process itself can be quite detailed, and we are not going to get that detailed here. The significant point is that these allocations must be made, they must have credible allocation bases to support them, and they should be applied consistently and transparently.

The End of the Book, But the Start of Using Your New Skills

You have made it to the end of our work together. We've covered significant ground in an effort to help you develop a sense of comfort and mastery over the financial statements. You have also seen some key analytical techniques that will help you identify and drill into problem areas, celebrate successes, and help guide your staff and board in meaningful ways.

Keep Reading

The appendices and glossary provide supplementary information that I think will be helpful in your further development as a financial leader.

I wish you well as you pursue your passion, and lead your organization toward a very successful future.

Glossary

Accounts payable - amounts owed to vendors of the organization, for which invoices have been received and entered into the accounting system. These will typically be paid in thirty days.

Accounts receivable - money owed to the organization in exchange for goods or services provided. Can be in the form of government contracts receivable or grants receivable. Different from unconditional promises to give, which are gifts that have been promised to the organization.

Accrual accounting - accounting method that records revenues and expenses when they are incurred, regardless of when cash is exchanged. Your organization should prepare financial statements using accrual, not cash, accounting.

Assets - something that the organization owns or is owed.

Balance sheet - provides cumulative, comprehensive financial information on your organization - as of a specific date - since the date of inception. Also called the statement of financial position.

Cash accounting - accounting method that records revenues and expenses only when cash is exchanged.

Current assets - cash and other assets that are expected to be converted to cash or used within a year.

Current liabilities - obligations that are due to be paid within one year.

Depreciation - a method of spreading the cost of a non-current asset over its useful life. This is a component of accrual accounting.

Fiscal year - a period that an organization uses for accounting purposes and preparing financial statements. The fiscal year may or may not be the same as a calendar year.

Functional expense - reporting expenses in one of three categories: programming, management (and administrative), or fundraising

Income statement - reports the organization's revenues and expenses for a specific range of time. Also called the statement of activities.

Liabilities - amounts owed to others by the organization. These can be in the form of current and non-current liabilities.

Liquidity - the availability of cash to pay bills as they come due.

Net assets - the cumulative amount left over after subtracting liabilities from assets on the statement of financial position. Reported by restriction, the unrestricted amount is technically the organization's reserve.

Net assets released from restriction - the result of spending funds in accordance with a donor's wishes.

Program expenses - also known as direct expenses, these are funds spent directly toward the goals and mission of the organization.

Restrictions

> **Unrestricted** - funds that have no stated purpose. Management and the board have the ability to utilize these funds as needed.

> **Temporary** - funds given to the organization with "strings" attached, in terms of purpose or time.

> **Permanent** - funds given to the organization whose principle must be maintained in perpetuity.

Statement of activities - reports the organization's revenues and expenses for a specific range of time. Also called the income statement.

Statement of cash flows - reports the sources and uses of cash in three categories: operating, investing, and financing.

Statement of financial position - provides cumulative, comprehensive financial information on your organization - as of a specific date - since the date of inception. Also called the balance sheet.

Statement of functional expenses - provides details of the three categories of expenses on the income statement: program, management, and fundraising.

Unconditional promises to give - donor gift money promised to the organization. Different from "accounts receivable," which is money owed to the organization in exchange for goods or services provided.

Unrestricted reserve - liquid, unrestricted assets that an organization can use at the discretion of management and the board.

Appendix I.

A Summary Report to Make Your Life Better

As we made our way through the four financial statements, we learned a number of analytical techniques that help call attention to important financial statement relationships. Through this learning process I asked that you keep your organization's statements close at hand to facilitate your analyzing the results. This was important for learning the material, and better understanding the relationships between the statements. Now, let's get the accounting staff to do the work for us, and present the information for our review.

The example on the following page is what I call the "secret sauce" of our joint learning experience. It is a summary chart of all the techniques we've covered, organized by financial statement. This is a snapshot of what we've learned together, and can also be thought of as a picture of your organization's financial health.

When looking at a report like this, the financial leader should be alert for, and ask for details such as:

• Is liquidity improving? What is the most important liquidity measure for my organization? What is our "comfort level" for days of cash on hand?

- Are we taking longer to collect our receivables? Is this a problem with our government grant invoices? Is the information correct on the statements sent to donors? Are we effectively communicating the need to convert receivables into cash?

- What is happening with the revenue mix? Are we moving toward revenues that require a higher cost of fundraising? Are our fundraising expenses effective?

- Are we generating or using cash? Where is the cash coming from, and going to?

Ideally, a chart like this will be completed and maintained by your accounting staff, and presented along with each month's financials. Also, this is easy to customize for your specific needs and organization. In fact, I believe this tool will be so useful that it should become the first page of your financial statements, followed by the more traditional statements. Ultimately the financial review documents should be whatever helps you and others to most effectively guide the organization's fiscal health.

Take a look, filled in with the results for All Good People, Inc.

ALL GOOD PEOPLE, INC.

Summary of Analytical Techniques

Fiscal Year Ended June 30, 2015, Actual and Budget

(with results for the year ended June 30, 2014)

Statement of Financial Position measures	2015 Actual	2015 Budget	2014 Actual
Current ratio	5.29	4.00	3.79
Quick ratio	1.05	1.00	0.87
Days of cash on hand	18.5	20.0	26.3
Days to collect receivables			
Total	70.5	75.0	80.4
Government contracts	79.9	80.0	100.0
Unconditional promises to give, net	61.1	55.0	59.2
Days of operating (unrestricted) reserve	(7.1)	(10.0)	(21.0)
Debt-to-equity	0.50	0.55	0.56
Statement of Activities measures			
Net margin	-2.4%	5.0%	0.4%
Mix of Functional expenses			

Program services	72.1%	75.0%	75.6%
Management and general	11.2%	12.0%	11.7%
Fundraising	16.7%	13.0%	12.7%
Total Expenses	100.0%	100.0%	100.0%
Mix of Revenue types			
Fundraising events revenue	24.8%	24.0%	23.8%
Government grants	49.5%	51.0%	51.8%
Contribution	24.5%	25.0%	24.4%
In-kind contributions	1.2%	0.0%	0.0%
Total Revenue and Support	100.0%	100.0%	100.0%
Fundraising Effectiveness			
Total Revenue	$5.86	$8.00	$7.90
Total Revenue, less Government Grant	$2.96	$4.00	$3.81
Statement of Cash Flows measures			
Cash flows from operating activities	(32,000)	71,000	256,000
Cash flows from investing activities			(74,000)
Cash flows from financing activities	(71,000)	(71,000)	(60,000)
Net Change in Cash and Cash Equivalents	(103,000)		122,000

Appendix II.

Reports that Provide Additional Details for the Statement of Activities

A. The Statement of Functional Income and Expenses is a report that takes the Statement of Functional Expenses and adds to it the income for each category. Here we have also detailed the program activities of the organization, as you can see that there are programs for adult education, youth service, and arts and culture. Now you can see more clearly where the organization has positive and negative changes in net assets.

ALL GOOD PEOPLE, INC.

Statement of Functional Income and Expenses
Fiscal Year Ended June 30, 2015

	Program Services			Supporting Services		
	Adult Education	Youth Services	Arts & Culture	Management and General	Fundraising	2015 Total
Fundraising events revenue, net of expenses ($125,000 in 2015 and $110,000 in 2014)	$	$	$	$	$1,550,000	$1,550,000
Government grants	1,490,000	1,606,000				3,096,000
Contributions					325,000	325,000
In kind contributions				75,000		75,000
Net assets released from restrictions	612,000	505,000	190,000			1,397,000
Total Revenue and Support	2,102,000	2,201,000	190,000	75,000	1,875,000	6,443,000

Salaries	1,261,000	1,322,000	76,000	365,000	567,000	3,591,000
Employee benefits and payroll taxes	265,000	278,000	15,000	73,000	113,000	744,000
Total Personnel	1,526,000	1,600,000	91,000	438,000	680,000	4,335,000
Professional fees						
(includes in-kind legal fees of $75,000)	161,000	156,000	41,000	186,000	82,000	626,000
Occupancy	31,000	28,000	12,000	12,000	16,000	99,000
Building and office supplies	45,000	27,000	19,000	4,000	21,000	116,000
Printing, publication and postage	26,000	25,000	20,000	5,000	55,000	131,000
Advertising	5,000	7,000	14,000		1,000	27,000
Program supplies	121,000	124,000	25,000		35,000	305,000
Food and refreshments	46,000	85,000	14,000	7,000	100,000	252,000
Equipment rental	3,000	3,000	16,000	2,000	4,000	28,000
Insurance	21,000	22,000	2,000	4,000	4,000	53,000
Repairs and maintenance	12,000	16,000	5,000	17,000	3,000	53,000
Interest	55,000	56,000	12,000	28,000	25,000	176,000
Depreciation	65,000	66,000	16,000	12,000	15,000	174,000
Bad debt					27,000	27,000
Bank Fees			2,000	2,000		2,000
Total Other Expenses	591,000	615,000	196,000	279,000	388,000	2,069,000
Total Expenses	2,117,000	2,215,000	287,000	717,000	1,068,000	6,404,000
Change in Net Assets	$(15,000)	$(14,000)	$(97,000)	$(642,000)	$807,000	$ 39,000

B. Functional Income and Expenses, by funding source: The previous statement showed that programs services comprises three programs, one of which is adult education. We continue to drill deeper into the statements, now seeing that the adult education program is actually funded by three grants, one each from the state, the city, and a foundation.

ALL GOOD PEOPLE, INC.

Statement of Functional Income and Expenses, by Funding Source
Adult Education Programming
Fiscal Year Ended June 30, 2015

	Adult Education			
	State Grant #1	City Grant #2	Foundation Grant #3	2015 Total
Fundraising Events Revenue, net of expenses ($125,000 in 2015 and $110,000 in 2014)	$	$	$	$
Government grants	826,000	664,000		1,490,000
Contributions				
In-kind contributions				
Net assets released from restrictions			612,000	612,000
Total Revenue and Support	826,000	664,000	612,000	2,102,000

				Total
Professional fees (includes in-kind legal fees up to $75,000)		99,000	62,000	161,000
Occupancy	14,000	12,000	5,000	31,000
Building and office supplies	18,000	14,000	13,000	45,000
Printing, publication and postage	4,000	8,000	14,000	26,000
Advertising			5,000	5,000
Program supplies	21,000	38,000	62,000	121,000
Food and refreshments	2,000	4,000	40,000	46,000
Equipment rental			3,000	3,000
Insurance	8,000	7,000	6,000	21,000
Repairs and maintenance	4,000	4,000	4,000	12,000
Interest	20,000	18,000	17,000	55,000
Depreciation	30,000	20,000	15,000	65,000
Bad debt				
Bank fees				
Total Other Expenses	**220,000**	**187,000**	**184,000**	**591,000**
Total Expenses	827,000	666,000	624,000	2,117,000
Change in Net Assets	$ (1,000)	$ (2,000)	$ (12,000)	$ 15,000

C. Income and Expenses, Actual versus Budget for a single funding source: Taking a look at only State Grant #1, we want to see how the actual results compared to the budget. This type of report should be available once the monthly books have been closed. This is critical to understanding the changes that occurred from the time of planning to the end of execution, for a year.

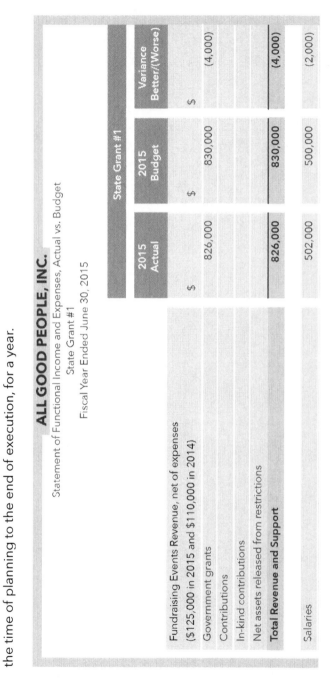

ALL GOOD PEOPLE, INC.

Statement of Functional Income and Expenses, Actual vs. Budget

State Grant #1

Fiscal Year Ended June 30, 2015

	State Grant #1		
	2015 Actual	2015 Budget	Variance Better/(Worse)
Fundraising Events Revenue, net of expenses ($125,000 in 2015 and $110,000 in 2014)	$	$	$
Government grants	826,000	830,000	(4,000)
Contributions			
In-kind contributions			
Net assets released from restrictions			
Total Revenue and Support	**826,000**	**830,000**	**(4,000)**
Salaries	502,000	500,000	(2,000)

Employee benefits and payroll taxes	105,000	100,000	(5,000)
Total Personnel	**607,000**	**600,000**	**(7,000)**
Professional fees			
(includes in-kind legal fees up to $75,000)	99,000	100,000	1,000
Occupancy	14,000	15,000	1,000
Building and office supplies	18,000	20,000	2,000
Printing, publication and postage	4,000	10,000	6,000
Advertising			
Program supplies	21,000	25,000	4,000
Food and refreshments	2,000	10,000	8,000
Equipment rental			
Insurance	8,000	10,000	2,000
Repairs and maintenance	4,000	10,000	6,000
Interest	20,000	15,000	(5,000)
Depreciation	30,000	15,000	(15,000)
Bad debt			
Bank fees			
Total Other Expenses	**220,000**	**230,000**	**10,000**
Total Expenses	827,000	830,000	
Change in Net Assets	$ (1,000)	$ 830,000	$ (1,000)

Stay in Touch With Brian

Sign up for news and updates: www.clearsightadvisors.co

LinkedIn: **https://www.linkedin.com/company/clear-sight-advisors-llc**

Twitter: **@clearsightadv**

Facebook: **@clearsightadv**

Remember, you can download all the statements from this book. I've also included a summary of all the formulas. Here's the link: **www.clearsightadvisors.co/premium**